MINECRAFT

D1766954

ENGLISH
OFFICIAL WORKBOOK
AGES 9-10

**JON GOULDING
AND DAN WHITEHEAD**

INTRODUCTION

HOW TO USE THIS BOOK

Welcome to an exciting educational experience! Your child will go on a series of adventures through the amazing world of Minecraft, improving their written English skills along the way. Matched to the National Curriculum for writing for ages 9–10 (Year 5), this workbook takes your child into fascinating landscapes where our heroes Zack and Nadia embark on building projects and daring treasure hunts…all while keeping those pesky mobs at bay!

As each adventure unfolds, your child will complete topic-based questions worth a certain number of emeralds . These can then be 'traded in' on the final page. The more challenging questions are marked with this icon ♥ to stretch your child's learning. Answers are included at the back of the book.

MEET OUR HEROES

An expert builder, Zack always thinks big! Whether he's planning a giant build of his own or seeking out incredible structures in remote corners of the world, he only wants experiences that will push him to the limit and force him to be the best he can. Often this means he finds himself in situations that are dangerous or scary, but his explorer's knowledge and best friend Nadia keep him safe. Well, most of the time…

Nadia is a fizzing ball of energy! She loves to invent new redstone creations and is always looking for rare materials to use in her next project. She would much rather get on with things than spend time planning them out, which leads her and Zack into some wild adventures. Always bright and optimistic, she doesn't let any challenge get her down, whether it's facing a terrifying new mob or exploring a spooky new biome.

First published in 2021 by Collins
An imprint of HarperCollins*Publishers*
1 London Bridge Street, London, SE1 9GF

HarperCollins*Publishers*
1st Floor, Watermarque Building, Ringsend Road, Dublin 4, Ireland

Publisher: Fiona McGlade
Authors: Jon Goulding and Dan Whitehead
Project management: Richard Toms
Design: Ian Wrigley and Sarah Duxbury
Typesetting: Nicola Lancashire at Rose and Thorn Creative Services
Minecraft skins courtesy of Claudia 'ZestyKale' Faye
Special thanks to Alex Wiltshire, Sherin Kwan and Marie-Louise Bengtsson at Mojang and the team at Farshore
Production: Karen Nulty

ISBN 978-0-00-846284-0
British Library Cataloguing in Publication Data.
A CIP record of this book is available from the British Library.
2 3 4 5 6 7 8 9 10
Printed in the United Kingdom

MIX
Paper from responsible source
FSC® C007454

This book is produced from independently certified FSC™ paper to ensure responsible forest management.

For more information visit: www.harpercollins.co.uk/green

CONTENTS

TRANSCRIPTION AND SPELLING

TONNES OF TIMBER

Need some wood for your crafting projects? The forest is where you should go. There are trees, trees and more trees as far as the eye can see!

REMAIN ALERT

The trees provide cover for enemy mobs like skeletons, zombies and creepers to sneak up on you. So, while you are hacking away with that axe, keep your eyes and ears open for unwanted visitors!

OBSIDIAN SEARCH

Zack and Nadia have big plans. After so many adventures together, they are finally going to build a Nether portal and explore the spooky and gloomy world of the Nether. It will be their most dangerous expedition yet, but first Zack has to leave his forest home to find enough obsidian to build the portal...

PREFIXES

A prefix is a letter or letters added to the beginning of a root word (a word with a clear meaning on its own). Adding a prefix changes the meaning of the word, but the spelling of the root word is unchanged. For example, the prefix *un-* can be added to the word *happy* to make the new word, *<u>un</u>happy*.

Zack has arranged to meet Nadia on the other side of the forest once he has the materials needed for the Nether portal. First he needs some obsidian and he uses his map to find a useful lava cave he had explored before. Help him to get off on the right foot by answering the following questions.

1

Draw lines to match each prefix to the correct word.

| un- | dis- | in- | re- | auto- | mis- | inter- |

| correct | heard | mobile | national |

| belief | turn | fair |

2

The prefix *in-* usually means *not*. However, in the highlighted words in the sentences below another prefix meaning *not* has been used. Explain how the spelling of the root word has led to *in-* being replaced by another prefix.

a)   It was **impossible** to imagine what lay ahead.

....

b)   It would be **irresponsible** to not prepare carefully.

....

c)   The writing on the map was **illegible**.

....

WORD ENDINGS -CIOUS AND -TIOUS

Words ending in *-cious* and *-tious* are often confused when spelling because they sound very similar. There isn't a spelling rule to cover all cases, but if the root word ends in *-ce* then *-cious* is usually used (for example: *vice – vicious*). If there are words in the word family with a *t* at the end or as part of the ending, then *-tious* is more likely to be used (for example: *ambition – ambitious*).

Zack checks his equipment. He has cooked chicken for health, his diamond pickaxe for mining the obsidian, and a bucket of water to pour on the lava.

1

Read each word and underline the *-cious* or *-tious* ending.

ambitious   suspicious   fictitious   malicious   vicious

2

At the end of each sentence, write the root word for each highlighted word.

a)   Zack was **ambitious** to build a portal.   ....

b)   The bucket was **spacious** and could carry lots of water. ....

c)   The cooked chicken was very **nutritious**.   ....

Zack sets off to the lava cave he had marked on his map. It is a long walk and he has to fight several skeletons along the way.

3

Choose the best word from the box to write in each sentence.

| nutritious | precious | conscious | cautious | suspicious |

a) Zack was so tired he was barely ....

b) He needed some .... food to help his health.

c) Zack would be mining .... obsidian ore very soon.

d) He needed to be .... because there were more hostile mobs about.

4

 Think about the word *fierce*. What happens when you add the *-cious* ending to it? Use a dictionary to help you.

....

....

WORD ENDINGS -CIAL AND -TIAL

The *-cial* ending is common after a vowel (for example: *artificial*) and *-tial* is usually used after a consonant (for example: *partial*). However, there are several exceptions.

Zack finds the cave and ventures inside. He knows the lava is deep underground and that the cave is likely to be home to lots of spiders. Help him to climb down by answering the following questions.

 1

Write the root word for each of the words below.

a) racial ....

b) partial ....

c) official ....

d) financial ....

2

Choose the best word from the box to write in each sentence.

essential	special	beneficial	confidential

a) It was .... that Zack was on the look-out for spiders.

b) His experience exploring the cave before would be extremely

....

c) Zack clutched his .... sword tightly.

Zack reaches the flowing lava river and prepares to pour his bucket of water onto it to create obsidian blocks.

3

Write the correct spelling for the underlined word in each sentence.

a) Zack's **inicial** job was to create the obsidian from lava. ....

b) It was **crutial** that he did not spill the water. ....

c) There was a **potencial** danger at every turn. ....

d) A spider appeared and this was not a **sotial** visit. ....

4

Think about the word *palace*. Would you add the *-cial* or the *-tial* ending to it to create an adjective? Explain why the choice of ending could be confusing when compared with other words. Use a dictionary to help you.

....

....

....

COLOUR IN HOW MANY EMERALDS YOU EARNED

9

ADDING SUFFIXES TO THE WORD ENDING *-FER*

Some words ending in *-fer* need the final *r* doubling when a suffix is added, but other words have the suffix added without any further changes. If the *-fer* part of the word is stressed (emphasised more) when saying the word aloud, the *r* is doubled (for example, *transfer* becomes *transferred* or *transferring*). When the *-fer* is not stressed, there is no change (for example, *confer* becomes *conference*).

Hissss! Zack pours the water onto the red-hot lava, turning it into obsidian. Now he just needs to get rid of this spider and he can start mining!

1

Choose the correct word from the box to write in each sentence.

infer	suffer	prefer	offer

a) Zack would .... to keep away from the spider.

b) The spider did not .... any other choice than to fight.

c) Nadia would make him .... if he didn't bring enough obsidian!

2

Read each word below. Underline the part of the word which is stressed when the word is said aloud. For example: *trans<u>fer</u>*

refer   prefer   differ

Zack defeats the spider and he starts chipping away at the obsidian blocks with his diamond pickaxe. It is hard work!

3

Add the *-ed* ending to the words in the box which then fit into the sentences below.

suffer	refer	transfer	offer	prefer

a) Zack .... the obsidian to his inventory.

b) He had .... an injury fighting the spider.

c) He .... to finish mining before healing himself.

d) His food .... excellent healing properties.

4

Complete the table below, ensuring that each word has the correct ending.

	Suffix -ed	Suffix -ing	Suffix -ence
prefer	preferred		
differ		differing	
refer			reference

COLOUR IN HOW MANY EMERALDS YOU EARNED

WORDS WITH SILENT LETTERS

A silent letter is used in the spelling of some words but it is a letter that is not pronounced and cannot be heard when the word is said aloud. Words with a silent letter can be tricky to spell.

Now he has enough obsidian blocks to build a Nether portal, Zack just needs a flint and steel to create the fire needed to activate it. He decides to leave the cave and explore the forest.

1

Write the silent letter found in each of the words below.

a) write ....

b) knot ....

c) gnome ....

d) what ....

e) autumn ....

f) comb ....

g) castle ....

h) guard ....

2

Underline the silent letter in the emboldened word and complete the sentences appropriately.

a) Zack was **calm** and ....

b) He stopped to **listen** and ....

c) There was no **doubt** it would ....

d) His iron **sword** ....

To craft a flint and steel, Zack needs an iron ingot and some flint from a gravel block. He searches the forest for anything useful.

3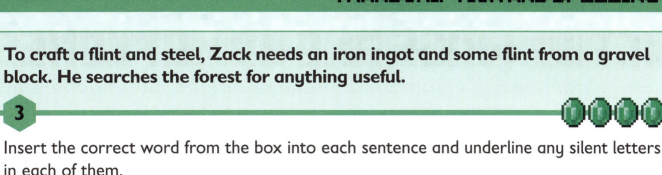

Insert the correct word from the box into each sentence and underline any silent letters in each of them.

| whistle | knee | climb | island |

a) Zack hurt his .... jumping down from a ledge.

b) He decided to .... a ladder to get a better view.

c) There was a lake with a small .... in the middle of it.

d) Zack could hear all sorts of sounds in the forest, including one noise that was like a

....

4

Read each of the pairs of words below. Complete each 'rule' to say which letter comes before or after the silent letter.

a) thumb, lamb

At the end of a word, ...

....

b) gnat, gnome

At the beginning of a word, ...

....

DICTIONARIES AND HOMOPHONES

A dictionary can be used to help with spelling and to find the meaning of words. It can be useful for checking that the correct homophone or near-homophone (words which sound the same or very similar) has been used. Knowing the first few letters of a word helps when looking for it in a dictionary because words are sorted in the alphabetical order of their first letter and, if this is the same, by the alphabetical order of their second letter, and so on.

Zack swims across the lake to the island. Maybe there will be something he needs there after all?

1

Write the six homophones below in alphabetical order.

proceed ....

precede ....

past ....

passed ....

prophet ....

profit ....

2

Circle the correct homophone in each given pair in the short passage below. Use a dictionary to check the meaning of each.

*Zack was thinking **aloud / allowed**. He had **herd / heard** a strange sound up ahead and*

*was now very **wary / weary** about going any **father / farther**.*

Zack arrives on the island and finds it is full of zombies! He draws his sword and starts battling!

3

Write sentences about Zack on the island using each of the homophones below.

a) guessed ....

b) guest ....

c) steal ....

d) steel ....

4

Use a dictionary to help you use each given word correctly in its own sentence.

a) descent ....

dissent ....

b) ascent ....

assent ....

COLOUR IN HOW MANY EMERALDS YOU EARNED

EI AND IE SPELLINGS

The spellings patterns *ei* and *ie* are often confused. Both spelling patterns often make the *ee* sound as heard in *peep* (for example: *ceiling* and *priest*). The spelling rule '*i before e except after c*' suggests that the *i* always appears before *e* (*ie*) unless it follows *c* in a word, in which case *e* comes before *i* (*ei*). There are a number of exceptions (such as *protein*) and these include words in which the *ie* does not make an *ee* sound (for example: *science* and *efficient*).

Suddenly, Zack hears a familiar voice. It is Nadia! She helps him to defeat the zombies then shows him where she had spotted some iron ore.

1

Shade in the four boxes containing words in which *ie* or *ei* makes the *ee* sound, as heard in *peep*.

height		ceiling		perceive	
	shriek		friend		priest

2

Choose the best word from the box to write in each sentence.

receive	relief	deceive	friend

a)   Zack was pleased to .... some help from Nadia.

b)   It was great to have a .... he could rely on.

c)   It was such a .... to be safe and out of danger.

Nadia takes Zack to a small cave with iron ore in its walls. Nadia places a cobblestone block on the cave's floor, so Zack can reach the ore and mine it. As they work, Nadia tells Zack about her adventures.

 3

Read the passage below. Add *ie* or *ei* correctly into each emboldened word.

Nadia told Zack that there had been some **misch**............**f** *in the village. A* **th**............**f** *had managed*

to **dec**............**ve** *the villagers, who* **bel**............**ved** *he was a good person. They were all* **rel**............**ved**

when the **ch**............**f** *culprit was caught.*

 4

Help Zack to use the word *seize* in a sentence. Create a sentence using this word (or this word with an *-ed* or an *-ing* ending).

....

....

COLOUR IN HOW MANY
EMERALDS YOU EARNED

USING THE HYPHEN

Some words need a hyphen when a prefix is added. This is often the case when the prefix ends with a vowel and the root word also begins with one (for example: *co-ordinate*). A hyphen is also used after *ex* and after *self* (for example: *ex-manager* and *self-respect*).

Now all Zack and Nadia need is some flint, and that is easily found by digging through gravel until they find some. They have everything they need!

 I

Choose the best hyphenated word from the box to write in each sentence.

co-operate	**ex-colleague**	**re-enter**	**self-confidence**

a) Nadia's friendship always improved Zack's ....

b) Nadia and Zack had learned to .... well.

c) They decided they needed to .... the cave to find flint.

2

A hyphen can also be used to prevent confusion. Read the sentence below and explain the difference in meaning between the two highlighted words.

*Zack had to **recover** his sword while Nadia had to **re-cover** their shelter with leaves.*

....

....

....

....

COLOUR IN HOW MANY EMERALDS YOU EARNED ⬦⬦⬦⬦⬦

ADVENTURE ROUND-UP

PURPLE-LIT PORTAL

Zack places his obsidian blocks in a rectangular shape to create the Nether portal's frame and Nadia uses the flint and steel to ignite its centre. There is an eerie whooshing sound as the portal activates. A swirling, purple vortex appears in the portal.

NOW TO THE NETHER!

When Zack and Nadia step through the portal, they will be transported to the creepy world of the Nether. The pair of them look at each other and nod. It is time. They take a deep breath and enter the portal...

VOCABULARY, GRAMMAR AND PUNCTUATION

NASTIES IN THE NETHER

Welcome to the Nether wastes! Or, more precisely, beware of the Nether wastes! This place is not somewhere you would want to come on holiday. Only mushrooms grow in this gloomy, red wasteland, and it is also home to lots of terrifying zombified piglins and magma cubes.

RICH PICKINGS

Despite the dangers, there are treasures and rare resources galore for those brave enough to cross over into this strange new realm.

SPOOKY START

Zack and Nadia emerge from the portal into the sinister dimension of the Nether. It is hot and spooky here, and they both gulp in fear. What have they let themselves in for? With no plan other than exploration, they swallow their anxiety and strike out into the vast blood-red terrain ahead of them...

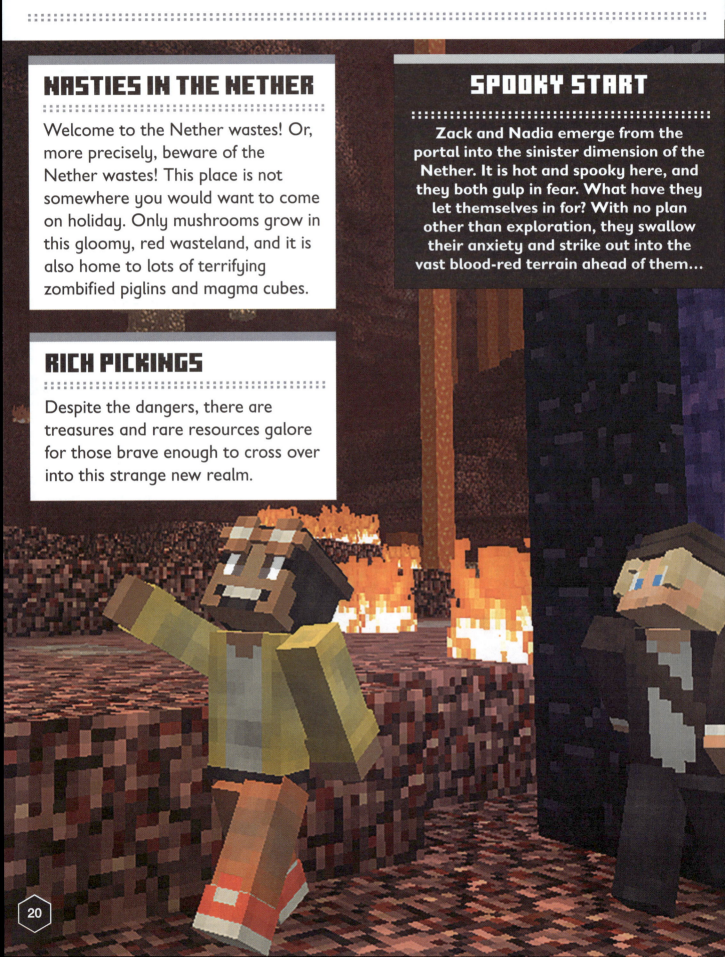

DIRECT SPEECH

Direct speech shows the words a character says. For example, *"I hope we don't see any piglins,"* whispered Nadia. The spoken words (underlined in this example) are enclosed by inverted commas with a comma placed after the last spoken word. They are followed by a reporting clause (*whispered Nadia*), which shows who was speaking (Nadia) and how that person spoke (whispering).

Zack and Nadia wander through the Nether wastes. The ground is made of netherrack, which crunches under their feet.

1

Add the missing punctuation to each sentence.

a) "We should look for rare resources " said Nadia

b) Will it be dangerous " asked Zack.

c) Only if we are careless, replied Nadia.

2

Rewrite each of the sentences below so that they use direct speech.

a) Zack told Nadia that he could see some Nether quartz ore in the distance.

....

....

b) Nadia advised Zack to keep his sword in his hand at all times.

....

....

VERB TENSE

Tense tells us when something has happened (past), is happening (present) or will happen (future).

Zack and Nadia set off towards the Nether quartz ore, but the sound of grunting and snorting distracts them. Piglins are approaching!

1

Tick the two sentences in which the underlined verbs are written correctly.

The piglins are <u>following</u> Zack.

Piglins <u>walking</u> all over the Nether wastes.

Nadia and Zack <u>was</u> on another adventure.

The adventurers <u>screamed</u> because it was so creepy.

2

Rewrite the two incorrect sentences from question 1, making sure that the verb is used correctly.

....

....

Nadia and Zack battle the piglins. Nadia knows about these creatures. "They only attack if you are not wearing gold armour!" she shouts.

3

Complete the table below, filling in the gaps with the correct use of the verb *to walk*. The first one has been done for you.

Tense		Example
Present	Simple present	Zack **walks**
	Present progressive	Zack is ....
Past	Simple past	Zack ....
	Past progressive	Zack was ....
	Present perfect	Zack has ....

4

Place the four words listed in the box into the correct places in the sentences.

Use the table from question 3 to help you.

has battling was battled

a) Nadia .... an aggressive piglin.
(present perfect)

b) Nadia .... an aggressive piglin.
(past progressive)

COLOUR IN HOW MANY
EMERALDS YOU EARNED

THE PERFECT TENSE

The present perfect tense talks about actions that started in the past and continue to the present. The word *have* or *has* is used before the past participle (often ending in *-ed*) of the main verb. For example, *Zack has already visited many biomes.*

The past perfect tense talks about events completed before something else happened. The word *had* is used before the past participle of the main verb. For example, *Zack had already visited many biomes when he arrived in the Nether wastes.*

Nadia and Zack finally defeat the piglins. The Nether is definitely a scary and dangerous place!

Write **past perfect** or **present perfect** after each sentence to show you understand each tense.

a)   The piglins have followed Zack. ....

b)   They had followed Nadia before. ....

c)   Nadia and Zack had battled hard against the piglins. ....

d)   Zack has listened to Nadia's advice. ....

e)   Lava had appeared ahead of them. ....

f)   Hostile mobs have been spawning all day. ....

There is Nether quartz ore everywhere! As Nadia mines it with her pickaxe, Zack quickly builds a shelter to keep them safe.

2

Complete each sentence with the correct form of the verb *to have*.

a) They .... walked for a long time.   (present perfect)

They .... walked for a long time.   (past perfect)

b) Nadia .... mined the Nether quartz ore.   (past perfect)

Nadia .... mined the Nether quartz ore.   (present perfect)

c) The shelter .... been built.   (present perfect)

The shelter .... been built.   (past perfect)

3

Write one **past perfect** and one **present perfect** sentence about Zack or Nadia.

a) Past perfect   ....

....

b) Present perfect   ....

....

COLOUR IN HOW MANY EMERALDS YOU EARNED

ADDING INFORMATION ABOUT NOUNS

When more information is given about a noun in a sentence, the writing almost always becomes more interesting. For example, a noun phrase such as *the sword* can be expanded by adding an adjective or two: *the heavy, shining sword.* Following a noun phrase, a prepositional phrase can add further information about time or place. For example, *the heavy, shining sword in the hands of Zack.*

As Zack and Nadia admire the Nether quartz inside their shelter, they hear a horrible shriek from outside. Oh no! An Enderman!

 1

Draw lines to join each sentence opener on the left with the most suitable prepositional phrase on the right.

Nadia heard the terrifying sound	across the vast Nether wastes.
Zack stood staring	outside of the shelter.
The Enderman lurked	from very nearby.
Nadia carried her inventory	on her back.

2

Insert the best adjective from the box in the space before the noun in each sentence.

mighty	awful	tough	lazy

a) Zack was prepared for a .... battle.

b) Nadia heard the .... sound.

c) She gripped her .... sword.

Zack and Nadia keep watch patiently, hoping the Enderman will leave them alone and not steal the blocks making up their shelter.

 3

Underline the noun phrase and circle the prepositional phrase in each sentence.

a) Nadia heard the noisy Enderman in the eerie gloom.

b) Zack placed the glittering Nether quartz in his inventory.

c) They had met many mobs during their adventures.

d) They hoped the menacing Enderman would go away before they left.

 4

Write two sentences about the Nether wastes, each with an expanded noun phrase (containing an adjective and a noun) followed by a prepositional phrase.

COLOUR IN HOW MANY
EMERALDS YOU EARNED

NOUNS AND PRONOUNS

Writing becomes repetitive and does not flow as well as it could for the reader if the same noun is used too often. For example: *Nadia held <u>Nadia's</u> sword tightly. <u>Nadia</u> saw Zack reach for <u>Zack's</u> weapon and <u>Nadia</u> knew that <u>Nadia and Zack</u> were in danger.* You can make improvements by using pronouns and possessive determiners (such as *my, your, his/her*) to replace repeated nouns. For example: *Nadia held <u>her</u> sword tightly. <u>She</u> saw Zack reach for <u>his</u> weapon and <u>she</u> knew that <u>they</u> were in danger.* This is much easier to read and gives better cohesion between the sentences.

It seems to take forever for the Enderman to drift away. Finally able to relax, Zack and Nadia stay in the shelter and talk about their adventure so far.

1

Show belonging in the sentences below by adding the most suitable possessive pronoun.

a) Zack and Nadia considered this one of the most dangerous adventures of

....

b) "Zack's inventory is emptier than ....," thought Nadia.

c) When Nadia gave him the Nether quartz, she told Zack it was now

....

d) They agreed to share whatever they found and both said, "The quartz is

...."

Nadia suggests they try mining deep into the netherrack to see if they can find a rare type of ore called ancient debris. Zack is keen but worried about the piglins.

2

Replace the emboldened nouns in the passage with the correct pronoun or possessive determiner.

The Nether wastes are full of danger because **the Nether wastes** *are full of piglins. The piglins*

scare Nadia because of the noise **the piglins** *make. Nadia kept* **Nadia's** *weapons close by* **Nadia** *at*

all times. Zack was also scared and **Zack** *did not want* **Zack and Nadia's** *adventure spoiled by a*

piglin or two. **Zack's** *sword was always ready and* **Zack** *was skilled at using* **the sword**.

3

♥ Write a sentence using each of the pronouns below.

a) yours ....

....

b) it ....

....

c) she ....

....

COLOUR IN HOW MANY
EMERALDS YOU EARNED

RELATIVE CLAUSES

Relative clauses add further information about a noun, a noun phrase or a proper noun (the name of something or someone) in a sentence. They are clauses 'related' to the noun. A relative clause is introduced by a relative pronoun such as *who, whose, which* and *that*. For example: *The sword <u>that</u> Nadia uses is sharp.*

Nadia and Zack leave the shelter behind and begin their search for ancient debris. Nadia digs while Zack keeps watch for enemies.

1

Underline the relative clause in each sentence.

a)   Nadia had a pickaxe that she used to dig into the netherrack.

b)   The piglins were enemies that Zack was wary of.

c)   That was the mob whose screams were the loudest.

d)   Zack was an adventurer who was a great fighter.

2

Underline the noun that the emboldened relative pronoun refers to.

a)   Nadia dropped the netherrack, **which** she had just mined.

b)   The zombified piglin's sword **that** it had once carried, lay on the floor.

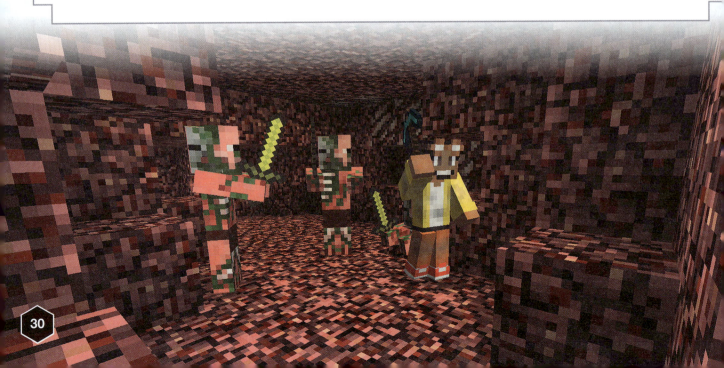

Nadia digs very deep and discovers a cave full of zombified piglins. Luckily, she knows that they won't attack unless provoked.

3

Circle the correct relative pronoun in each sentence.

a) Nadia's sword **who / that** she crafted herself, was sharp.

b) Zack is the hero **that / who** is great with a bow.

c) The Nether wastes biome, **which / what** they are in, is a difficult environment.

d) Nadia and Zack, **who / which** are great friends, support each other.

4

Add a suitable relative clause to each sentence.

a) Nadia stared at the zombified piglins ....

....

b) They saw some ancient debris in the wall ....

....

ADVERBS AND MODAL VERBS

Adverbs are used to give more information about verbs. They can be used to indicate the degree to which something is true or happens (how much, how often or how well). For example: *Zombies are <u>quite</u> dangerous. Nadia walked <u>extremely</u> quickly.*

Modal verbs can be used to show the degree of possibility – whether something is certain (will happen), probable (likely to happen) or possible (might happen). For example: *They <u>will</u> escape. They <u>could</u> escape. They <u>might</u> escape.*

Zack and Nadia spot some unusual blocks. Is that ancient debris? To reach it, they will have to cross a pool of lava.

Underline the adverb in each sentence that shows the degree of possibility.

a) There was possibly a way around the lava.

b) Perhaps that was not ancient debris after all.

c) Nadia was fairly confident they had found it.

d) Zack was extremely excited.

2

Complete the table to show whether each sentence is **certain** or **not certain** to happen or have happened. Place one tick in each row.

	Certain	Not certain
Nadia had certainly dug very deep.		
Maybe the ancient debris would be useful.		
Zack definitely did not want to see any more enemies.		
It will be difficult to complete this mission.		
They could leave here with some great resources.		

It is ancient debris! Nadia knows it is one of the toughest ores and will be hard work to mine, even with her diamond pickaxe.

3

Underline the modal verb in each sentence.

a) Nadia said she would be ready to craft with the ancient debris.

b) It looked like it might take a long time to dig out.

c) They should have used stronger tools.

d) Zack knew they could make use of it.

4

Choose a suitable adverb or modal verb to complete each sentence.

a) Zack .... see the piglins approaching. (certain)

b) They .... run away immediately. (certain)

c) .... they would not spot them. (not certain)

d) Nadia .... have stopped but she kept going. (not certain)

e) This is an adventure they .... never forget. (certain)

COLOUR IN HOW MANY
EMERALDS YOU EARNED

ADVERBIALS OF TIME, PLACE AND NUMBER

Adverbs and adverbial phrases or clauses are often used to tell the reader when (time), where (place) and the order (number) of things that happen. For example:

They stood <u>in the vast Nether wastes</u>.   (place)

They were ready <u>as the piglins appoached</u>.   (time)

<u>Secondly</u>, they built a shelter.   (number)

Zack and Nadia start to dig their way out and have to quickly jump out of the way as lava pours into their tunnel. They are under a lava lake!

Place a tick in the correct column of the table for each sentence to show whether it indicates **place**, **time** or **number**.

	Place	Time	Number
The lava gushed in as soon as Zack broke the blocks.			
First, they jumped away from the lava.			
Nadia ran back down the tunnel.			
Zack stood on a block in the middle of the lava.			

2

Choose the best adverb from the box to insert in each sentence.

away	frequently	into	finally

a) .... they dug around the lava.

b) The lava flowed .... from them.

c) Zack walked .... the new exit he had dug.

They emerge from their tunnel next to the lava lake. There is a strange creature walking through the boiling molten rock. Zack knows what it is. A strider!

3

Draw lines to join each of the sentence starters on the left with a suitable adverbial on the right. Choose a different adverbial each time.

They wanted to go	early in the day.
They had looked for ore	across the lava lake.
They had left home	after escaping lava in the tunnel.
They needed to rest	everywhere.

4

Write two sentences which tell the reader that Nadia checked she had a saddle in her inventory then helped Zack fight more piglins. Use adverbials of place, time and number.

....

....

....

....

COMMAS

Commas have several uses. They can be used to separate items in a list. For example: *Nadia fought zombies, ghasts, piglins and spiders.* They are also often placed after a fronted adverbial, and are used in direct speech. For example: *Nadia said, "I have my sword ready."* They are also used to clarify meaning for the reader. For example: *"Time to eat Zack," said Nadia* has a much different meaning to *"Time to eat, Zack," said Nadia.*

Zack explains that if they had a warped fungus and a fishing rod, they could control the strider and ride it like a horse. Nadia loves that idea!

1

Complete the list with three additional items after each sentence starter below.

a) Only fungus grows in the Nether, but other biomes can grow trees, ...

....

b) Nadia had visited several places including the plains, ...

....

2

How have the commas been used in each of the sentences below? Choose your answers from the options in the box.

after a fronted adverbial	with direct speech	to clarify meaning

a) After finding a warped forest biome, they looked for fungus.

....

b) They now had to concentrate on eating, dangerous mobs and finding shelter.

....

c) "I hope we can ride a strider," said Zack.

....

They manage to find some warped fungus growing in the warped forest. It is green and orange and smells funny!

3

Rewrite each sentence below, using a comma to clarify meaning.

a) "You must hurry up and hide Nadia," called Zack.

....

b) Most of the time travellers had lots of fun exploring.

....

c) Nadia likes fighting cake and mining.

....

4

For each of the sentences in question 3, write a short explanation of why a comma is needed.

a) ....

....

b) ....

....

c) ....

....

COLOUR IN HOW MANY EMERALDS YOU EARNED

37

PARENTHESIS

Parenthesis is indicated by brackets, commas or dashes. It refers to a word, phrase or clause added into a sentence to give extra information or to clarify a point. If the word (or words) are removed, what is left still makes sense. For example: *Nadia and Zack, two great adventurers, were on yet another mission.* The words *two great adventurers* give additional information. The sentence still makes sense without them.

Nadia carefully approaches the strider. The warped fungus is dangling from the fishing rod as bait.

I

Underline the parenthesis in each of these sentences.

a)   Nadia's fishing rod (a gift from Zack) was ready for action.

b)   The strider, tall and strange, came closer to her.

c)   Zack and Nadia – best friends forever – hoped they could control it.

d)   The lava lake, a red-hot hazard, kept them at a distance.

e)   The strider came up to Nadia (who was standing safely on the ground).

f)   In front of them, stretching into the distance, was nothing but lava.

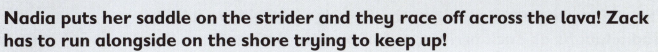

Nadia puts her saddle on the strider and they race off across the lava! Zack has to run alongside on the shore trying to keep up!

2

When a clause is inserted into a sentence between commas, it is known as an embedded clause. Relative clauses (see page 30) can be embedded clauses. Underline the embedded clause in each of these sentences.

a) The strider, which Nadia was riding, moved through the lava very quickly.

b) Zack, who is a fast runner, struggled to keep up.

c) Nadia, who sat upon the strider, loved the exciting ride over the lava.

3

Rewrite each sentence using the best relative clause from the box.

> **which was so fast on lava**   **which was so hot and fiery**
>
> **who had been on many adventures**

a) Zack and Nadia were ready to explore a new Nether biome.

....

....

b) The strider ran very slowly on land.

....

....

c) The lava lake came to an end at a creepy valley.

....

....

The strider comes to a halt at the far edge of the lava lake. Nadia laughs as Zack arrives, out of breath. Before them is a soul sand valley, one of the scariest and most dangerous biomes of all.

4

Place a tick or a cross in the box after each sentence to show if parentheses have been used correctly or not.

a)   Even Nadia who (was brave) was unsure of the sinister valley.

b)   The friendly – strider which Nadia rode – would not leave the lava.

c)   Zack, his sword in hand, wanted to continue onwards.

d)   The valley – a dark and scary place – was their next destination.

5

Rewrite the two incorrect sentences from question 4, ensuring the parentheses are used correctly.

....

....

....

....

....

....

COLOUR IN HOW MANY EMERALDS YOU EARNED

ADVENTURE ROUND-UP

DANGER, DANGER

Their adventure in the Nether has already been wild and scary – and now Nadia and Zack are about to enter a new and even more dangerous place.

GOODBYE TO THE STRIDER

Nadia is sad to see her friendly strider leave but it cannot follow them into the valley and she knows it would be safer in its lava lake home. The two heroic friends nod to each other. They are ready for whatever comes next...

COMPOSITION

FRIGHTS IN THE FOG

You may come across all kinds of scary situations on your adventures, but nothing is scarier than finding yourself in a soul sand valley. These barren Nether biomes are shrouded in creepy blue fog, with giant fossils and ruins poking from the lifeless ground. Just in case that isn't scary enough, the air is filled with wails and whispers.

SPOOKY SURROUNDINGS

Nadia and Zack stay close together as they step into the soul sand valley and begin to explore. Eerie shapes can be seen through the mist and spooky cries seem to come from all directions. They both wish they were back at home in the forest, but the portal is a long way away now so they press ahead, ready for anything.

VALLEY VALUABLES

There is amazing loot to be found in a soul sand valley but only the bravest will survive to discover it!

AUDIENCE AND PURPOSE

Before and during writing, you must consider and remember who the text is for, and what the text is for; in other words, the audience and the purpose. Is the intended audience an adult or a child? Is it being written to entertain (usually fiction, such as a story) or is it being written to provide information (usually non-fiction, such as a recipe book, instructions or facts about a subject)?

The mist seems to grow thicker and clings to the ground as they walk. To distract themselves from the creepiness, Nadia and Zack wonder how they could write up this adventure when they get home.

Nadia and Zack intend to write stories and information books based on their adventures. Tick the correct boxes in the table below to show the audience and the purpose of each text. The first one has been done for you.

Book title	Audience		Purpose	
	Adult	**Child**	**Inform**	**Entertain**
Recipes for plants found in biomes	✓		✓	
A young person's guide to mining				
Family book of creepy tales				
Biome adventures without kids				

2

Draw lines to join the text extract on the left to the purpose of the writing on the right.

The illagers raided the village with a force of 3 pillagers, a vindicator and a ravager.	Adventure story
Hoglins are dangerous mobs found in the Nether.	Newspaper report
The brave adventurer climbed higher. It was dangerous but he was nearly there now.	Information text

ORGANISING NON-FICTION WRITING

Any piece of writing of more than a few sentences should be in paragraphs. Each paragraph should have a different focus or idea. Non-fiction texts also use a number of other features to organise the information for the reader. Headings and subheadings can be used for paragraphs and groups of paragraphs, and information can be presented in tables, images and diagrams.

The soul sand valley is swarming with aggressive mobs. Nadia and Zack have to be on their guard constantly and they fight many battles as they explore.

Nadia and Zack fight many hostile mobs in the Nether. These include 36 skeletons, 5 Endermen, 23 ghasts, 7 piglins and 17 magma cubes.

a) Present the information given above in this table.

Hostile mob	Number encountered

b) Explain why a table such as this might be used.

....

....

Nadia and Zack would be more scared if they did not have information from a book that Zack has brought. It tells them what to expect in the Nether.

 2

The main headings (and sections) in Zack's book are the names of different biomes. Each section has a number of subheadings. One subheading in each section is 'Passive Mobs', containing information about the passive mobs found in each biome. Write a suitable subheading for each of the following pieces of information.

Information	Subheading
a) Skeletons, ghasts and others with information about where they spawn and how dangerous they are.	....
b) Information about plants that grow in the biome.	....
c) Information about building materials in the biome.	....

 3

Write a paragraph of at least three sentences briefly describing a biome you know, or a biome you have made up. Use the name of the biome as a subheading.

Subheading: ....

....

....

....

....

....

....

....

ORGANISING FICTION WRITING

Without good organisation, fiction writing can become very confusing for the reader. Paragraphs are very important. For example, when introducing characters, you can use separate paragraphs for each of them. Another paragraph may describe something about the setting. The paragraphs must be organised into an order which helps tell the story in a sensible way.

The mist grows so thick that Nadia and Zack lose sight of each other. Nadia whirls around, trying to find her friend in the gloom.

 1

Label each short paragraph with one of the choices from the box to show what part of the story it comes from.

character description	setting description	plot

a) Eerie soul fires stretched before her, blue and cold. Around them, a grey mist echoed with disembodied voices.

....

b) Whatever it was attacked quickly and without warning. She instantly swung her sword at the mysterious shape that had appeared beside her.

....

c) Her hand was badly cut but she held her sword with as much determination as ever. She was clearly familiar with fighting.

....

d) A Nether fossil poked from the soul sand on which she stood. Mushrooms were the only things growing in this very strange environment.

....

Meanwhile, Zack finds himself alone in a sinister corner of the valley. Dark basalt columns rise into the sky. Out of nowhere, four ghasts attack, shooting fireballs at poor Zack!

2

Write two paragraphs, of at least three sentences each, about what happens to Zack. The first paragraph should describe the attack, and the second should describe how Nadia comes to the rescue.

COLOUR IN HOW MANY
EMERALDS YOU EARNED

COHESION

Cohesion in writing means making sure that clauses, sentences and paragraphs link together well, making the text easier and more interesting to read and understand. Indicating time with words such as *first, then, next* and *finally* helps to sequence the events. Conjunctions such as *because, so,* and *when* help to link ideas. Adverbs such as *quickly* and *slowly* are useful devices to introduce an idea, and adverbial phrases (for example, *as rapidly as they could*) give more information to the reader. Pronouns also help with flow by avoiding repetition of nouns.

The ghasts are defeated but the spine-chilling cries from the mist tell Nadia and Zack that more are on the way. They are completely lost now!

 1

Underline the pronouns and circle the conjunctions in the text below.

Zack moved quickly because he knew there was great danger. Nadia followed Zack so she could

help him. They knew this was a scary adventure as the loud screech came again.

2

Rewrite the following passage to improve cohesion. Insert the best conjunctions from the box to join sentences, and replace the underlined words with pronouns.

because	but	and

Nadia saw Zack ahead. .... <u>Nadia</u> knew they were almost there. A huge column

towered above <u>Nadia and Zack</u>. .... they were not afraid. Zack was ready for battle.

.... <u>Zack</u> had trained so hard.

....

....

....

....

Zack and Nadia trudge across the soul sand (which slows them down), desperate to get away from the mobs and find a way out of this horrible valley.

 3

Read each paragraph below.

> *Suddenly, a ghast appeared from nowhere, but it was not quick enough for Nadia. First, she drew her sword and took a step to the side. Next, she swung violently at the attacker because she had to escape. As the ghast was struck, Nadia knew that she was safe again.*

> *A ghast appeared from nowhere. It was not quick enough for Nadia. She drew her sword. Nadia took a step to the side. Nadia swung violently at the attacker. Nadia had to escape. The ghast was struck. Nadia knew that she was safe again.*

☐ ☐

a) Place a tick below the paragraph with the best cohesion between sentences and ideas.

b) Give three reasons for your choice above.

....

....

....

 **4**

Rewrite the short paragraph below, improving cohesion.

Zack had always liked adventures. Zack thought they were exciting. Zack went on his first adventure when he was very young. Zack started collecting weapons when he was old enough. Zack got a wooden sword. Zack then got a diamond sword. Zack started to train hard. Zack became a very good fighter.

....

....

....

....

WRITING ABOUT CHARACTERS

Your character descriptions need to be effective to enable the reader to visualise what they look like and understand their behaviour. The characters need to be believable and fit with the story idea and plot. The things a character says and does can also help the reader to form an impression of that individual.

As they run, Nadia stumbles and falls down a steep slope hidden in the mist. Zack tries to help her but skeletons appear at the top of the slope!

Draw lines to join each piece of text to what it is telling the reader about that character.

A skeleton crept around the top of the ledge, shooting arrows at Zack to stop him reaching Nadia. It looked like a sinister smile spread across its bony face.	scared
"Don't worry," called Zack, "I'll get down there to you." Using his pickaxe, he quickly dug steps downwards into the gloom.	brave
"I knew all sorts of crazy things would happen in the Nether but that's what makes adventures fun," said Nadia.	enthusiastic
"Please don't leave me," she pleaded. "I need your help to get out of here and there are too many mobs to face by myself!"	cruel

After escaping from the skeletons, Nadia and Zack find themselves on the shore of another sizzling lava lake. Out of the mist, they see something approaching...

2

Draw lines to match each part of this character description to what it is telling the reader about that character (in this case, the strange creature that is approaching Nadia and Zack).

The creature was tall, with a wide flat face, and small glowing eyes.

An icy chill surrounded this being and its large ominous shape gave it a menacing presence.

A strange creature approached through the mist. It was impossible to make out the details.

introduction to the character

how the character looks

more interesting information

3

Write one or two sentences for each part of a description for Nadia or Zack.

Introduction to the character

....

....

How they look

....

....

Speech – make the character say something to show they are a good person

....

....

WRITING ABOUT SETTINGS

Good description of a setting is important to help the reader understand where a story is happening. They should be able to visualise the setting and get a good idea of what it is like there. Describing a setting is not just about what a place looks like, but also its sounds and smells.

The shape is purple and shivering. The mist parts and Zack and Nadia are surprised to see it is their strider! It had followed them into this creepy valley to help!

Think about the soul sand valley and write eight adjectives to describe it. Consider the sights, sounds, smells and how it makes you feel.

....

....

....

....

2

Answer these questions about the soul sand valley. Use your adjectives from question 1 to help you.

a) What can you see?

....

b) What can you hear?

....

c) How does it feel to be there?

....

They are so happy to see their friendly strider. It is even still wearing Nadia's saddle! Nadia climbs onto its back and Zack follows as it leads them out of the gloom.

3

Put together your ideas from questions 1 and 2 to write a short paragraph (three or four sentences) describing the soul sand valley.

....

....

....

....

....

....

....

4

Think of another biome or setting (it could be one you make up). Think of three adjectives to describe that place and then compose a paragraph to describe it.

Adjectives: ....

Description: ....

....

....

....

....

EDITING AND PROOFREADING

Before somebody reads your piece of writing, it should go through the processes of editing and proofreading. Editing can help to improve the grammar and vocabulary of the text, making sentences sound more effective and adding more interesting words. Proofreading means checking for spelling and punctuation mistakes in words and sentences to ensure they make sense.

The strider brings them to the edge of a cliff. Below is a crimson forest and, in the distance, a vast, black, crumbling structure. Zack knows what this is!

1

Edit the text below by improving the highlighted words, then rewrite it. Adjust the sentence lengths to help the text flow better.

Zack **be** excited because they **has** found a bastion remnant which is **a old** structure that is full of **bad** monsters as well as **nice** treasure. **Zack** warned Nadia that this would be a **hard** place to explore and **unsafe** but **Zack and Nadia** knew it would be worth the **danger**.

....

....

....

....

2

Underline the spelling and punctuation mistakes in the passage below. Rewrite the text with these mistakes corrected.

Zack and nadia say thank you to there strider frend and carefully, climb down the cliff? The crimson forest streches before them The forest is dark and threatning.

....

....

....

COLOUR IN HOW MANY EMERALDS YOU EARNED

ADVENTURE ROUND-UP

READING UP ON THE REMNANTS

Standing at the edge of the crimson forest, Zack and Nadia can see the top of the bastion remnant looming over the trees. Zack takes his book about the Nether from his inventory. He finds the chapter on bastion remnants. He and Nadia gulp nervously. Inside these dark walls will be piglins and deadly piglin brutes, as well as magma cubes guarding the treasure room.

NO TURNING BACK

"We have come so far," reflects Zack.

"We can't turn back now," replies Nadia.

With pounding hearts, they enter the murky forest…

CREATIVE WRITING

LET'S GET RED-Y!

Crimson forests are some of the Nether's most beautiful and creepy biomes. As the name suggests, they are deep red in colour. Even the fog here is red!

SPOOKY SIGHTS

Packs of wild hoglins roam the crimson forest and gigantic fungi grow everywhere, with sinister weeping vines hanging from them. You may also find spooky structures spawning here, such as the fabled bastion remnant.

FOREST FORAY

Nadia and Zack are pleased to be out of the soul sand valley, with its eerie howls and blinding mists. Will the crimson forest be any less scary? They are about to find out!

STORY PLANNING

A story needs characters, a setting, and a plot (what actually happens in the story). For example, Nadia and Zack (characters) visit the Nether (the setting) to mine ore and find treasure (the plot).

Nadia and Zack enter the crimson forest, staying alert for the sound of any dangerous mobs. Zack asks Nadia to tell him a story to keep his spirits up.

Consider a story about an adventure in the Nether. Answer the following questions to help you think about a basic story plan.

a) Who is in the story (who is the main character or characters)?

....

b) Where is the story set?

....

c) What is it that your characters want to do in the story?

....

d) What dangers/problems could they face?

....

e) Will they succeed?

....

STORY WRITING 1: OPENING

Once the basic ideas have been planned, the story opening (also sometimes known as the 'introduction' or 'beginning') can be written.

Zack likes the sound of the story. He asks Nadia to tell him more about the main character – they sound cool!

Think about the main character(s) of your story and answer the following questions. Only do this for one character here, but you always need to make sure you think of the same questions for other key characters too.

a) What does the character look like? Think about their size and how they move too.

....

....

b) What is the character like? Are they a kind, good person?

....

....

c) Why are they going on this adventure?

....

....

d) How do they feel?

....

....

Nadia and Zack step on warped fungus blocks that squish and squelch beneath their feet. Yuck! Zack collects some of this curious material.

2

Think about the setting of your story.

a) Where is the story set?

....

b) What is it like there?

....

c) What is good and what is bad about the setting?

....

3

Write the beginning to your story by using the ideas you have formed while answering each part of questions 1 and 2. Remember to say each sentence aloud before you write to check that it makes sense. Remember to use different paragraphs (for example, for the characters and for the setting).

....

....

....

....

....

....

....

....

COLOUR IN HOW MANY EMERALDS YOU EARNED

STORY WRITING 2: DEVELOPING THE PLOT

A very simple story plot, with no action or exciting events, might not be very interesting for the reader. Introducing a problem (such as the characters being attacked by hostile mobs or getting lost) allows more excitement to be included.

Nadia is still telling her story when Zack pauses. He can hear something snuffling and grunting close by.

How does your plot start? Think about what happens before a problem is introduced. This is sometimes known as the 'build-up'. The character might have started their adventure — maybe walking along, noticing different things along the way, climbing over rocks — and it can be exciting but not yet a problem for them. Consider having two events or different pieces of action (which will form two separate paragraphs when you write your ideas as sentences later).

Event or action	What the characters do and how they feel

A pack of hoglins has caught up with Nadia and Zack. There is a steep cliff in front of them and hostile mobs behind them. They are trapped!

2

Think about a problem that the character(s) in your story could face. This needs to be something that could stop them achieving their aims in the story. It might be a hostile mob or another danger, or getting lost, or bad weather. Make notes in the table below to help you plan the problem. At this point, there is no need to say how they solve the problem.

Problem	Why is this a problem?
How do the characters know they have a problem?	**How do the characters feel?**

3

Write the build-up and problem parts of your story by using the ideas you have written for questions 1 and 2.

....

....

....

....

....

....

....

....

COLOUR IN HOW MANY EMERALDS YOU EARNED

STORY WRITING 3: RESOLUTION AND ENDING

Once you have introduced a problem in a story, you need to describe how it is solved. What do the characters do to escape, survive or get back on track to complete their aims? This is known as the 'resolution' (to the problem) and it comes before the story ending. A story ending should tell the reader if (and how) the characters complete their aims and how they feel.

1

Think about the problem you have written about on the previous page. Answer the questions below to help you to plan the resolution to your story.

a) What do the characters need to do? Is there more than one thing they need to do?

....

....

b) Is there anything they need to help them (for example, weapons or skills)?

....

....

c) What key events take place in solving the problem? Have at least one and, if possible, two or three events.

....

....

d) How do the characters feel while they are trying to solve the problem? Think about how you might feel as this may help you to imagine the feelings of the characters.

....

....

Zack remembers a useful fact from his book about the Nether. He quickly places the warped fungus he picked on the ground. The hoglins hate it and won't come near!

 2

Consider your story ending. Add notes to the table below to help you plan some ideas.

What happens?	Was the mission a success?	How do the characters feel?

 **3**

Write your resolution, saying how the problem is solved, followed by your story ending. Use your notes and answers from questions 1 and 2, and remember to use paragraphs.

....

....

....

....

....

....

....

....

....

NON-FICTION WRITING 1

When considering non-fiction writing, make sure you have a clear idea of what information you want to give to the reader. Also make sure you carefully think about the methods you will use to present the information and the order in which it will be given.

With the hoglins distracted by the warped fungus, Nadia and Zack scramble up the cliff and find themselves standing in front of the bastion remnant.

1

Which of the following might you include in a non-fiction text? Tick three options.

Subheadings ☐   Facts ☐

Made-up characters ☐   Tables ☐

2

Explain why you might use subheadings in a non-fiction text.

....

....

....

The bastion remnant is huge and menacing. Zack quickly pulls out his book to help them to understand what lies inside.

3

Write three ideas you could include in a text about the Nether and rare loot.

....

....

....

4

Consider the sections of a book about the Nether and rare loot. Put the four sections below in the correct order. Write the numbers 1–4 in the boxes.

Final summary ☐   Further detail about the Nether ☐

Introduction ☐   Information about loot in different biomes ☐

COLOUR IN HOW MANY EMERALDS YOU EARNED

NON-FICTION WRITING 2

Non-fiction writing needs careful planning and organisation. It is a good idea to use headings and subheadings to tell the reader what each section is about.

Nadia is fascinated by the way everything in the Nether is made from completely different materials to those she is used to seeing. She decides she will write about mining when they get home.

 1

Nadia is planning to write a text about mining and ore. The introduction needs to give an overview of what mining is. It does not need much detail as that will come in later sections. Answer the questions below to give ideas for different parts of the introduction.

What is mining?	Why do you need to mine?	What is ore?

2

Use your ideas from question 1 to write an introduction to mining under this subheading:

Introduction

....

....

....

....

....

Nadia and Zack creep inside the bastion remnant. The echoing halls and passageways are made from gloomy blackstone. Nadia mines some of it.

Using tables in non-fiction writing helps to summarise large amounts of information. Complete the table below with information that could be given after the introduction, showing the key features of some ores. You may need to do some of your own research to gather the information you need.

Ore name	Tool for mining	Uses
Coal		
Iron		
Gilded blackstone		

Nadia wants to give the reader more detailed information about mining. Write a paragraph (or two) with further information under this subheading:

Mining

....

....

....

....

....

....

....

....

....

NON-FICTION WRITING 3

Non-fiction writing often gives some information in lots of detail. To do this, you need to use more facts and have a very good understanding of your topic.

The bastion remnant is made from quartz blocks and is guarded by piglins. Zack distracts them while Nadia gets to work mining.

1

In her book, Nadia decides to write in more detail about ores in the Nether. She will need at least two paragraphs – one introducing the Nether and another explaining the ores found there. Complete the table below with ideas for these two paragraphs. You may need to do some of your own research to gather the information you need.

What is the Nether?	Information about Nether ores
	Nether quartz Nether gold Ancient debris

2

Use the ideas from your completed table in question 1 to write information under this subheading:

The Nether and Nether Ores

Nadia also finds basalt, gold and glowstone in the bastion remnant. Her inventory is very heavy now!

3

Non-fiction texts often have a concluding or a summary paragraph at the end. For Nadia's text about mining and ores, it will be a brief recap of information covered in the text.

Complete the sentences below to give a basic structure for the summary paragraph.

a) Mining is the method used to ....

b) Ores are ....

c) The Nether is ....

d) Nether ores are ....

4

Using your ideas from the sentences in question 3, write a final paragraph summarising the information in Nadia's text.

....

....

....

....

....

....

....

EDITING

Editing is an opportunity to make changes to the sentences you have written, including to the grammar and vocabulary. This is important because it helps you to check that the writing makes sense and can be understood by the reader. Additional information can also be inserted at this stage to make the writing more interesting or exciting.

Zack and Nadia find the treasure room but it is full of piglin brutes and fiery, hot magma cubes pouring out of a spawner!

1

Draw lines to match each pair of sentences to the correct description of how the original sentence has been edited.

Original: The treasure room was hot. It was dangerous.
Edited: The treasure room was hot and dangerous.

Improving vocabulary

Original: They grabbed their swords when they saw magma cubes.
Edited: When they saw magma cubes, they grabbed their swords.

Joining sentences

Original: Suddenly, Zack hit the spawner. It broke.
Edited: Suddenly, Zack destroyed the spawner.

Using a fronted adverbial

2

Make further edits to each of the edited sentences in question 1 by adding more information for the reader.

....

....

....

....

With the magma cubes defeated, and the spawner destroyed, Nadia and Zack are exhausted. As they get their breath back, they reflect on this amazing adventure.

3

Choose one of your own sections of story writing from pages 58–63 and read and edit that piece. Think about any vocabulary and ideas that you could improve or add to, and any sentences you could change.

4

Choose one of your own pieces of non-fiction writing from pages 66–69 and read and edit that piece. Think about whether the information makes sense, any words or sentences you could improve, and whether all the information makes sense.

COLOUR IN HOW MANY EMERALDS YOU EARNED

PROOFREADING

It is important to proofread your writing to check for any spelling mistakes and missing punctuation. This will make it more enjoyable and easier for the reader to understand.

Nadia and Zack defeat the furious piglins and fill up their inventories with gold blocks and loot from the treasure room's chests.

 I

Proofread each section of fiction and non-fiction text you have written in this section of the book. Find eight mistakes that you have spotted during your proofreading, noting what the mistake was and how you would change it. If you cannot find eight mistakes, do some further editing by changing some of the vocabulary for even better words. Note the original word and what you are changing it to.

Mistake (or word)	Change

COLOUR IN HOW MANY EMERALDS YOU EARNED

ADVENTURE ROUND-UP

NETHER CONCLUSION

It has been a long and sometimes scary adventure, but Nadia and Zack have bravely explored the Nether, faced its many dangers and earned all the treasure they have found.

FINDING THE WAY HOME

Now Zack and Nadia just have to find their way back to the portal to get home again. That is a whole new story, and maybe one you can help them to tell…

ANSWERS

Page 5

1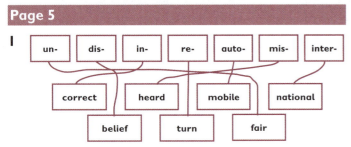

[1 emerald each: 'un-' can also join to 'heard']

2 a) The answer should acknowledge that if the root word begins with p, the prefix is *im-*. [1 emerald]

b) The answer should acknowledge that if the root word begins with r, the prefix is *ir-*. [1 emerald]

c) The answer should acknowledge that if the root word begins with l, the prefix is *il-*. [1 emerald]

Pages 6–7

1 amb**itious**   susp**icious**   fict**itious**
ma**licious**   vi**cious**   [1 emerald each]

2 a) ambition   [1 emerald]
b) space   [1 emerald]
c) nutrition   [1 emerald]

3 a) conscious   [1 emerald]
b) nutritious   [1 emerald]
c) precious   [1 emerald]
d) cautious   [1 emerald]

4 The answer should acknowledge that *fierce* becomes *ferocious*, with the 'i' in fierce dropped, and an 'o' added before the ending *-cious*.   [1 emerald]

Pages 8–9

1 a) race   [1 emerald]
b) part   [1 emerald]
c) office   [1 emerald]
d) finance   [1 emerald]

2 a) essential   [1 emerald]
b) beneficial   [1 emerald]
c) special   [1 emerald]

3 a) initial   [1 emerald]
b) crucial   [1 emerald]
c) potential   [1 emerald]
d) social   [1 emerald]

4 The answer needs to acknowledge that it would be expected that the -ce ending would require the -cial adding, but it is in fact -tial that needs adding to create 'palatial'.   [1 emerald]

Pages 10–11

1 a) prefer   [1 emerald]

b) offer   [1 emerald]
c) suffer   [1 emerald]

2 re**fer**   pre**fer**   **dif**fer   [1 emerald each]

3 a) transferred   [1 emerald]
b) suffered   [1 emerald]
c) preferred   [1 emerald]
d) offered   [1 emerald]

4

	Suffix -ed	Suffix -ing	Suffix -ence
prefer	preferred	preferring	preference
differ	differed	differing	difference
refer	referred	referring	reference

[1 emerald each]

Pages 12–13

1 a) w   b) k   c) g   d) h
e) n   f) b   g) t   h) u   [1 emerald each]

2 The correct letter should be underlined as below. Sentences will vary but must make sense.
a) ca**l**m   b) lis**t**en
c) dou**b**t   d) s**w**ord   [2 emeralds each]

3 a) **k**nee   b) clim**b**
c) is**l**and   d) w**h**is**t**le   [1 emerald each]

4 a) The answer should acknowledge that a silent 'b' at the end of a word is preceded by 'm'.   [1 emerald]

b) The answer should acknowledge that a silent 'g' at the start of a word is followed by 'n'.   [1 emerald]

Pages 14–15

1 passed   past   precede
proceed   profit   prophet
[1 emerald each]

2 aloud   heard   wary   farther   [1 emerald each]

3 a)–d) Answers will vary but must use each word correctly in a full sentence which makes sense.
[1 emerald each]

4 Answers will vary but each should use the given word correctly. **Examples:**
a) The descent was steep and dangerous.
[1 emerald]

She showed her dissent by walking away.
[1 emerald]

b) They made their first ascent of the mountain.
[1 emerald]

He gave his assent to the plan.   [1 emerald]

Pages 16–17

1 shriek   ceiling   perceive   priest
[1 emerald each]

2 a) receive   [1 emerald]

b) friend [I emerald]

c) relief [I emerald]

3 mischief   thief   deceive

believed   relieved   chief

[I emerald each]

4 Sentences will vary but must contain the word 'seize', 'seized' or 'seizing' used correctly. **Example:**
Zack **seized** his sword and ran towards the zombie.

[I emerald]

Page 18

1 **a)** self-confidence [I emerald]

b) co-operate [I emerald]

c) re-enter [I emerald]

2 The answer should acknowledge that 'recover' means to find or get back his sword, while 're-cover' means to put a further covering of leaves on the shelter.

[I emerald each]

Page 21

1 **a)** "We should look for rare resources⟨,⟩" said Nadia⟨.⟩

[I emerald]

b) ⟨"⟩Will it be dangerous⟨?⟩" asked Zack. [I emerald]

c) ⟨"⟩Only if we are careless,⟨"⟩ replied Nadia.

[I emerald]

2 Answers may vary slightly. Ensure that direct speech is used and punctuated correctly. **Examples:**

a) "I can see some Nether quartz ore in the distance," said Zack. [I emerald]

b) "Keep your sword in your hand at all times," advised Nadia. [I emerald]

Pages 22–23

1 The piglins are following Zack. ✓ [I emerald]

The adventurers screamed because it was so creepy. ✓

[I emerald]

2 Piglins **walked** all over the Nether wastes. [I emerald]

Nadia and Zack **were** on another adventure.

[I emerald]

3 Present progressive – Zack is walking. [I emerald]

Simple past – Zack walked. [I emerald]

Past progressive – Zack was walking. [I emerald]

Present perfect – Zack has walked. [I emerald]

4 **a)** has battled [2 emeralds]

b) was battling [2 emeralds]

Pages 24–25

1 **a)** present perfect **b)** past perfect

c) past perfect **d)** present perfect

e) past perfect **f)** present perfect

[I emerald each]

2 **a)** have, had [2 emeralds]

b) had, has [2 emeralds]

c) has, had [2 emeralds]

3 Answers will vary. Ensure each sentence is grammatically correct. **Examples:**

a) Nadia had been on an adventure. [I emerald]

b) Zack has been on an adventure. [I emerald]

Pages 26–27

1

Nadia heard the terrifying sound	across the vast Nether wastes.
Zack stood staring	outside of the shelter.
The Enderman lurked	from very nearby.
Nadia carried her inventory	on her back.

[I emerald each]

2 **a)** tough [I emerald]

b) awful [I emerald]

c) mighty [I emerald]

3 **a)** Nadia heard <u>the noisy Enderman</u> (in the eerie gloom.) [I emerald]

b) Zack placed <u>the glittering Nether quartz</u> (in his inventory.) [I emerald]

c) They had met <u>many mobs</u> (during their adventures.) [I emerald]

d) They hoped <u>the menacing Enderman</u> would go away (before they left.) [I emerald]

4 Answers will vary. Ensure each uses an expanded noun phrase and a prepositional phrase and is punctuated correctly. **Examples:**
The bleak landscape stretched beyond them.
Nadia saw the dangerous Enderman and ran across the Nether wastes. [Up to 2 emeralds per sentence]

Pages 28–29

1 **a)** theirs [I emerald]

b) mine [I emerald]

c) his [I emerald]

d) ours [I emerald]

2 they; they; her; her; he; their; His; he; it [I emerald each]

3 Answers will vary. Ensure each uses the pronoun correctly. **Examples:**

a) If you find the ore, it is yours to keep. [I emerald]

b) The Enderman was terrifying and it was angry.

[I emerald]

c) Nadia would return when she had the treasure.

[I emerald]

Pages 30–31

1 **a)** that she used to dig into the netherrack [I emerald]

b) that Zack was wary of [I emerald]

c) whose screams were the loudest [I emerald]

d) who was a great fighter [I emerald]

2 **a)** netherrack [I emerald]

b) sword [I emerald]

3 **a)** that   **b)** who

   c) which   **d)** who   [1 emerald each]

4 Answers will vary. Each must contain a relative clause. **Examples:**

   a) Nadia stared at the zombified piglins that were approaching.   [1 emerald]

   b) They saw some ancient debris in the wall which they were about to climb.   [1 emerald]

Pages 32–33

1 **a)** possibly   **b)** Perhaps

   c) fairly   **d)** extremely   [1 emerald each]

2 Nadia had certainly dug very deep. (certain)

Maybe the ancient debris would be useful. (not certain)

Zack definitely did not want to see any more enemies. (certain)

It will be difficult to complete this mission. (certain)

They could leave here with some great resources. (not certain)   [1 emerald each]

3 **a)** would   **b)** might

   c) should   **d)** could   [1 emerald each]

4 Answers will vary. Ensure the word used shows a 'certain' or 'not certain' event as indicated.

Examples:

   a) will   **b)** must   **c)** Perhaps

   d) could   **e)** will   [1 emerald each]

Pages 34–35

1

	Place	Time	Number
The lava gushed in as soon as Zack broke the blocks.		✓	
First, they jumped away from the lava.			✓
Nadia ran back down the tunnel.	✓		
Zack stood on a block in the middle of the lava.	✓		

[1 emerald each]

2 **a)** Finally   [1 emerald]

   b) away   [1 emerald]

   c) into   [1 emerald]

3 Answers will vary but each complete sentence must make sense. **Examples:**

They wanted to go	early in the day.
They had looked for ore	across the lava lake.
They had left home	after escaping lava in the tunnel.
They needed to rest	everywhere.

[1 emerald each]

4 Answers will vary but each sentence must use at least one adverbial. **Example:**

First, Nadia checked she had a saddle in her inventory. She then took out a weapon as she went to help Zack fight more piglins.   [1 emerald for each sentence]

Pages 36–37

1 Answers will vary. Ensure correct use of commas.

Examples:

   a) Only fungus grows in the Nether, but other biomes can grow trees, flowers, pumpkins and melons.   [1 emerald]

   b) Nadia had visited several places including the plains, ocean, beach and dark forest.   [1 emerald]

2 **a)** after a fronted adverbial   [1 emerald]

   b) to clarify meaning   [1 emerald]

   c) with direct speech   [1 emerald]

3 **a)** "You must hurry up and hide, Nadia," called Zack.   [1 emerald]

   b) Most of the time, travellers had a fun time exploring.   [1 emerald]

   c) Nadia likes fighting, cake and mining. [1 emerald]

4 Answers may vary but should indicate the following:

   a) to ensure that the spoken words are telling Nadia to hide, rather than that Nadia should be hidden   [1 emerald]

   b) to ensure the sentence is not about time travellers   [1 emerald]

   c) to show that Nadia likes fighting and cake, not fighting cake   [1 emerald]

Pages 38–40

1 **a)** (a gift from Zack)   [1 emerald]

   b) , tall and strange,   [1 emerald]

   c) – best friends forever –   [1 emerald]

   d) , a red-hot hazard,   [1 emerald]

   e) (who was standing safely on the ground)   [1 emerald]

   f) , stretching into the distance,   [1 emerald]

2 **a)** which Nadia was riding   [1 emerald]

   b) who is a fast runner   [1 emerald]

   c) who sat upon the strider   [1 emerald]

3 **a)** Zack and Nadia, who had been on many adventures, were ready to explore a new Nether biome.   [1 emerald]

   b) The strider, which was so fast on lava, ran very slowly on land.   [1 emerald]

   c) The lava lake, which was so hot and fiery, came to an end at a creepy valley.   [1 emerald]

4 **a)** ✗   **b)** ✗   **c)** ✓   **d)** ✓   [1 emerald each]

5 Even Nadia (who was brave) was unsure of the sinister valley.   [1 emerald]

The friendly strider – which Nadia rode – would not leave the lava.   [1 emerald]

Page 43

1

Book title	Audience		Purpose	
	Adult	Child	Inform	Entertain
Recipes for plants found in biomes	✓		✓	
A young person's guide to mining		✓	✓	
Family book of creepy tales	✓	✓		✓
Biome adventures without kids	✓		✓	

[2 emeralds] (A young person's guide to mining)
[3 emeralds] (Family book of creepy tales)
[2 emeralds] (Biome adventures without kids)

2

The illagers raided the village with a force of 3 pillagers, a vindicator and a ravager.	Adventure story
Hoglins are dangerous mobs found in the Nether.	Newspaper report
The brave adventurer climbed higher. It was dangerous but he was nearly there now.	Information text

[1 emerald each]

Pages 44–45

1 a)

Hostile mob	Number encountered
Skeletons	36
Endermen	5
Ghasts	23
Piglins	7
Magma cubes	17

[1 emerald for each row]

b) The answer should acknowledge that a table makes the information easier to look at. **[1 emerald]**

2 Answers will vary but should fit with the described information. **Examples:**

a) Hostile Mobs **[1 emerald]**
b) Plants **[1 emerald]**
c) Building Materials **[1 emerald]**

3 Answers will vary. Ensure that the sentences make sense and are correctly punctuated. This paragraph can refer to any biome. **Example:**
The soul sand valley is a creepy and dangerous place. Deadly mobs roam and a blue fog hangs over the ground. Nether fossils poke out of the soul sand.

[1 emerald for each sentence up to a maximum of 3]

Pages 46–47

1 a) setting description **[1 emerald]**
b) plot **[1 emerald]**
c) character description **[1 emerald]**
d) setting description **[1 emerald]**

2 Each sentence in each paragraph should be correctly constructed. Each paragraph should contain the required information. **[1 emerald for each sentence up to a maximum of 6]**

Pages 48–49

1 Zack moved quickly (because) he knew there was great danger. Nadia followed Zack (so) she could help him. They knew this was a scary adventure (as) the loud screech came again. **[1 emerald each]**

2 Nadia saw Zack ahead **and** she knew they were almost there. A huge column towered above them **but** they were not afraid. Zack was ready for battle **because** he had trained so hard. **[1 emerald each]**

3 a) The first paragraph should be ticked. **[1 emerald]**
b) Answers will vary but could include:
use of pronouns   use of adverbial phrases
use of conjunctions

[1 emerald each up to a maximum of 3]

4 Answers will vary. Ensure pronouns have been used to avoid repetition of 'Zack'. Conjunctions could also be used. **[1 emerald each for up to six changes]**
Example: Zack had always liked adventures **because he** thought they were exciting. **He** went on his first adventure when he was very young. Zack started collecting weapons when he was old enough **and he** got a wooden sword. **He** then got a diamond sword **and** started to train hard. Zack became a very good fighter.

Pages 50–51

1

A skeleton crept around the top of the ledge, shooting arrows at Zack to stop him reaching Nadia. It looked like a sinister smile spread across its bony face.	scared
"Don't worry," called Zack, "I'll get down there to you." Using his pickaxe, he quickly dug steps downwards into the gloom.	brave
"I knew all sorts of crazy things would happen in the Nether but that's what makes adventures fun," said Nadia.	enthusiastic
"Please don't leave me," she pleaded. "I need your help to get out of here and there are too many mobs to face by myself!"	cruel

[1 emerald each]

2

The creature was tall, with a wide flat face, and small glowing eyes.	introduction to the character
An icy chill surrounded this being and its large ominous shape gave it a menacing presence.	how the character looks
A strange creature approached through the mist. It was impossible to make out the details.	more interesting information

[1 emerald each]

3 Answers will vary. Each part should give different information about the character. **[1 emerald for each part]**

Pages 52–53

1. Answers will vary. **Examples:**

creepy	foggy	eerie	deadly
dangerous	scary	strange	musty

[1 emerald each]

2. **a)–c)** Answers will vary. Ensure that each sentence relates to the given prompt and contains a suitable adjective. **[1 emerald each]**

3. Each sentence in the paragraph should be correctly constructed. Each should relate to the soul sand valley (and be in more detail than the description written to answer question 3 on page 45).

[1 emerald for each sentence up to a maximum of 3]

4. Answers will vary. **[1 emerald for each adjective; 1 emerald for each sentence up to a maximum of 3]**

Page 54

1. Answers will vary but each highlighted word should be changed with suggestions in bold in the example below. An example of a change to the sentence structure is underlined.

Zack **was** excited because they **had** found a bastion remnant, which is **an ancient** structure that is full of **evil** monsters and **wonderful** treasure. **He** warned Nadia that it would be a **difficult** place to explore. It would also be **dangerous** but **they** knew it would be worth the **risk**. **[1 emerald for each change up to a maximum of 12]**

2. Zack and nadia say thank you to there strider frend and carefully, climb down the cliff? The crimson forest streches before them_ The forest is dark and threatning.

Zack and Nadia say thank you to their strider friend and carefully climb down the cliff. The crimson forest stretches before them. The forest is dark and threatening. **[1 emerald for each corrected mistake]**

Page 57

1. **a)–e)** Answers will vary. It is important that each one answers the given question. **[1 emerald each]**

Pages 58–59

1. **a)–d)** Answers will vary. It is important that each one answers the given question. **[1 emerald each]**

2. **a)–c)** Answers will vary. It is important that each one answers the given question. **[1 emerald each]**

3. Answers will vary. Ideally there should be a paragraph about the character(s) and a paragraph about the setting, with up to 3 emeralds (three sentences) for each paragraph, building on the ideas from questions 1 and 2. **[Up to 6 emeralds]**

Pages 60–61

1. Answers will vary. Each event or action must be an early part of the story (not a major event) and consideration should be given to how the character(s) act and feel. **[1 emerald for each completed section of the table]**

2. Answers will vary. The problem idea should be sufficient to have the potential to cause big issues for the character(s). **[1 emerald for each completed section of the table]**

3. Answers will vary. Ideally there should be a paragraph (or two) for the build-up and another for the problem, all based on the ideas from questions 1 and 2. Each paragraph is worth up to 2 emeralds depending on the quality of the sentences.

[Up to 4 emeralds]

Pages 62–63

1. **a)–d)** Answers will vary. It is important that each one answers the given question.

[1 emerald each]

2. Answers will vary. The ending idea should be considered and answer the three questions provided. **[1 emerald for each completed section of the table]**

3. Answers will vary. Ideally there should be a paragraph (or two) for the resolution and another for the ending, all based on the ideas from questions 1 and 2. Each paragraph is worth up to 2 emeralds depending on the quality of the sentences.

[Up to 4 emeralds]

Pages 64–65

1. Ticked: Subheadings; Facts; Tables **[1 emerald each]**

2. The answer should acknowledge that subheadings help to organise the text **[1 emerald]** and make information easier to retrieve **[1 emerald]**.

3. Answers will vary. Ensure the ideas make sense.

[1 emerald for each idea]

4.

Final summary	4	Further detail about the Nether	3
Introduction	1	Information about loot in different biomes	2

[1 emerald each]

Pages 66–67

1. Answers will vary. **Examples:**

What is mining?	Why do you need to mine?	What is ore?
Digging for ore	Because ores are very useful	Materials that can be used for many things

[1 emerald each]

2 Answers will vary. Ensure the response includes information from the notes in question 1.

[1 emerald for each sentence up to a maximum of 3]

3 Answers will vary. It is not necessary for the answers to give the exact tools and uses as in Minecraft but some research could help with the answer.

[1 emerald for each completed row]

4 Answers will vary. Ensure the response includes information from the notes in question 3.

[1 emerald for each idea up to a maximum of 3]

Pages 68–69

1 Answers will vary. It is not necessary for the answers to be authentic but some research could help with the answer.

[1 emerald for each completed section of the table]

2 Answers will vary. Ensure the response includes information from the notes in question 1.

[1 emerald for the Nether and 1 for ores]

3 **a)–d)** Answers will vary. Each completed sentence must make sense and use information from questions 1 and 2.

[1 emerald each]

4 Answers will vary. Sentences should be correctly constructed and contain the information from the previous answer.

[1 emerald for each piece of information]

Pages 70–71

1 Boxes joined as follows:

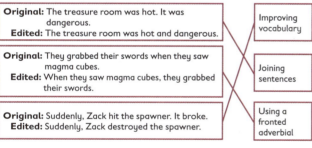

[1 emerald each]

2 Answers will vary.

[1 emerald for an additional piece of information for each sentence]

3 Answers will vary.

[1 emerald for each change up to a maximum of 4]

4 Answers will vary.

[1 emerald for each change up to a maximum of 4]

Page 72

1 Answers will vary.

[1 emerald for each change up to a maximum of 8]

TRADE IN YOUR EMERALDS!

Exploring the Nether was definitely a creepy adventure! Remember the sinister, misty soul sand valley? And the spooky bastion remnant? Thankfully Zack and Nadia had their friendly strider to help them – and you, of course! Thank you!

Now it's your turn. Imagine you are going on your own Minecraft adventure.

Add up all the emeralds you earned throughout this book, and decide what to buy from the trader to help you on your way.

Write the total number of emeralds you earned in this box:

HMMM?

SHOP INVENTORY

- FEATHER FALLING ENCHANTED BOOTS: 35 EMERALDS
- NETHERITE HELMET: 35 EMERALDS
- NETHERITE CHESTPLATE: 40 EMERALDS
- NETHERITE BOOTS: 30 EMERALDS
- DIAMOND SWORD: 25 EMERALDS
- DIAMOND PICKAXE: 20 EMERALDS
- PIERCING CROSSBOW: 20 EMERALDS
- SHIELD: 15 EMERALDS
- CAKE: 20 EMERALDS
- GOLDEN CARROT: 15 EMERALDS
- RABBIT STEW: 20 EMERALDS
- POTION OF REGENERATION: 30 EMERALDS
- POTION OF SWIFTNESS: 25 EMERALDS
- POTION OF NIGHT VISION: 25 EMERALDS
- TOTEM OF UNDYING: 50 EMERALDS

That's a lot of emeralds. Well done! Remember, just like real money, you don't need to spend it all. Sometimes it's good to save up.